GREAT OLYMPIC MOMENTS

Michael Hurley

Heinemann
LIBRARY

Chicago, Illinois

www.heinemannraintree.com
Visit our website to find out more information about Heinemann-Raintree books.

To order:

☎ Phone 888-454-2279

🖳 Visit www.heinemannraintree.com to browse our catalog and order online.

Edited by Kate de Villiers and Laura Knowles
Designed by Richard Parker
Picture research by Liz Alexander
Production by Camilla Crask
Originated by Capstone Global Library Ltd
Printed and bound in China by CTPS

15 14 13 12 11
10 9 8 7 6 5 4 3 2 1

Library of Congress Cataloging-in-Publication Data
Hurley, Michael, 1979-
  The Olympics : great olympic moments / Michael Hurley.
    p. cm.—(The Olympics)
  Includes bibliographical references and index.
  ISBN 978-1-4109-4123-7—ISBN 978-1-4109-4129-9 1.
Olympics—History. I. Title.
  GV721.5.H87 2012
    796.48—dc22   2010049496

Acknowledgments
We would like to thank the following for permission to reproduce photographs: Alamy pp. **16** (© Associated Sports Photography), **4 left** (© Mary Evans Picture Library); Corbis pp. **10** (© Bettmann), **4 right** (© How Hwee Young/epa); Getty Images pp. **7** (Central Press/Hulton Archive), **9** (Shaun Botterill /Allsport), **11** (Popperfoto), **12** (Steve Powell), **13** (Mark Carwell/AFP), **17** (Jerry Cooke/Sports Illustrated), **18** (Pascal Pavani/AFP), **21** (Romeo Gacad/AFP), **23** (Keystone /Hulton Archive), **25** (Tony Duffy); Press Association Images p. **15** (AP Photo/Rusty Kennedy), Reuters p. **19** (Bruno Domingos).

Cover photograph of Derartu Tulu and Elana Meyer reproduced with permission of Getty Images/John Iacono/Sports Illustrated.

Every effort has been made to contact copyright holders of material reproduced in this book. Any omissions will be rectified in subsequent printings if notice is given to the publisher.

Disclaimer
All the Internet addresses (URLs) given in this book were valid at the time of going to press. However, due to the dynamic nature of the Internet, some addresses may have changed, or sites may have changed or ceased to exist since publication. While the author and publisher regret any inconvenience this may cause readers, no responsibility for any such changes can be accepted by either the author or the publisher.

Contents

Some words are shown in bold, **like this**. You can find them in the glossary on page 30.

World of Olympics

The Olympic Games are based on the games that were held every **Olympiad** (four years) in **ancient Greece**. The Olympics have been held every four years since 1896, except during the two World Wars (1914–1918 and 1939–1945).

The Olympics feature athletes from around the world competing against each other in various different sports. Track and field events include sprinting, high jump, and javelin. There are also indoor events, such as swimming, cycling, and gymnastics. Other popular Olympic sports include soccer, tennis, and hockey. There are 38 different sports in total.

Olympic athletes' clothing has changed a lot. Take a look at these **marathon** runners from 1896 (above) compared to athletes in 2008 (right).

There are both Summer and Winter Olympic Games. The Winter Olympics are also held every four years, two years after the Summer Games. The sports in the Winter Olympics are very different. They include downhill and cross-country skiing, ice-skating, and bobsled.

Athletes with disabilities take part in the **Paralympic Games**. These take place every four years in the same country that hosts the Olympics. Athletes compete in a variety of sports.

Over the years there have been many great moments at the Olympics. However, there have also been some shocking and controversial moments.

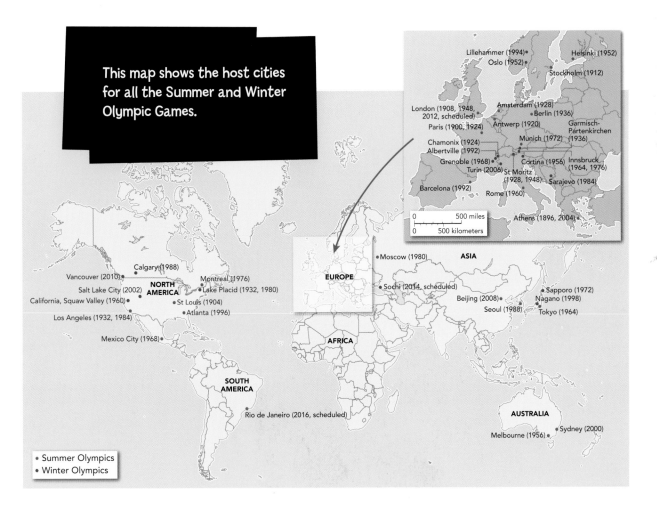

This map shows the host cities for all the Summer and Winter Olympic Games.

Amazing Moments

Every Olympic Games includes some amazing moments. The achievements of individuals can inspire and excite audiences around the world. From the bizarre to the heroic, these moments are remembered as part of Olympic history.

Eric the eel

In 2000 Eric Moussambani competed in the Sydney Olympics. The swimmer from Equitorial Guinea in Africa was not used to swimming more than 50 meters (160 feet). At the Olympics he had to swim 100 meters (330 feet). He was also the only person in the pool after other competitors were **disqualified** for false starts. The crowd cheered on Moussambani as he slowly finished his race and became an Olympic star. Later he said, "I could hear them cheering and it helped me to get to the end." His unusual swimming style earned him the nickname "Eric the eel."

Recovering from tragedy

Dan Jansen's sister died from leukemia a few hours before he competed at the 1988 Winter Olympics. The U.S. speed skater was the favorite to win gold, but he fell during the race. Days later he fell again in another race. It was too difficult for him to compete after such a tragic loss.

At the 1994 Olympics in Lillehammer, Norway, Jansen won a gold medal in speed skating and dedicated his win to his sister. The crowd applauded as he took his young daughter with him on his victory lap. His daughter was named Jane, after his sister.

Muhammad Ali (second from the right) was only 18 years old when he won a gold medal for boxing at the 1960 Olympics in Rome. Ali went on to become perhaps the greatest boxer in history and one of the most recognizable sportsmen in the world.

Usain Bolt

Winning the 100-meter Olympic title is a fantastic achievement. To win Olympic gold and break the world record is extremely special. Jamaican sprinter Usain "Lightning" Bolt did both at the 2008 Olympics in Beijing, China. Bolt was so far ahead of the other competitors in the 100-meter dash that he even slowed down as he crossed the finish line!

Cathy Freeman

The sight of Australian Cathy Freeman running in her green and gold hooded suit is one of the most memorable Olympic moments. Freeman was under intense pressure to win the 400-meter gold at the Sydney Olympics in 2000. It was a very close race, but in the final stretch Freeman took the lead, and she won by several meters. (A meter is just a bit longer than a yard.) The crowd in the Olympic stadium went wild!

Five gold medals

At the Sydney Olympics in 2000, Steve Redgrave became the first British athlete to win a gold medal at five **consecutive** Olympics. As part of two-man and four-man rowing teams, Redgrave proved himself to be one of the greatest athletes of all time. Redgrave and his teammates had to push themselves to the limit to win in Sydney. With only a short distance left, it looked as though they would be denied gold, but a final push helped them to win by just over half a second!

Steve Redgrave holds up his fifth Olympic gold medal for rowing. His haul of five gold medals makes him one of the greatest Olympians of all time.

Controversial Moments

In the history of the Olympics, some athletes have had to perform in difficult and unfair circumstances.

Shock for Hitler

The 1936 Olympics were held in Berlin, Germany. At the time, Adolf Hitler was the German leader. He wanted to use the Olympics to show how skilled and powerful German athletes were compared to those from other countries. Hitler's plan did not work. The outstanding performance of the 1936 Olympics came from Jesse Owens, an African-American athlete. Owens won four gold medals.

Jesse Owens leads the other competitors as he races toward another gold medal at the 1936 Olympics.

Racial differences

Incredibly, when Jesse Owens returned to the United States he did not receive much attention. At that time black people were treated differently from white people. This was known as **segregation**. At the 1968 Olympics in Mexico, two U.S. medal winners used the medal ceremony to highlight the fact that black people were still being treated differently in their country. After they received their medals, they each raised one fist wearing a black leather glove. The gloves represented the black people's fight for **equality** in the United States.

U.S. athletes Tommie Smith (middle) and John Carlos make their protest at the medal ceremony in 1968.

Skater attack!

Before the 1994 Winter Olympics, U.S. ice skater Nancy Kerrigan was assaulted and injured. It was later proved that she was attacked by someone hired by the ex-husband of another U.S. ice skater, Tonya Harding. Harding was worried about losing to her rival. Kerrigan recovered enough to compete and won a silver medal. Harding finished in eighth place.

Surprise Results

Often the team or athletes who are expected to win do take home the Olympic medals. Sometimes, however, the Olympics can produce a surprise result.

Miracle on ice

One of the most surprising results happened when the United States beat the **Soviet Union** at ice hockey in 1980. The Soviet Union was expected to win. Ice hockey was a sport they had **dominated** for many years. The United States was the **underdog**. By the end of the second period, the U.S. team was losing 3–2. But in the third period, the U.S. team started to play faster and more aggressively and scored twice to take a 4–3 lead. They held back the Soviet team for the last ten minutes of the match and won. The U.S. players and their fans were overjoyed. The result was so unexpected that it was called "the miracle on ice."

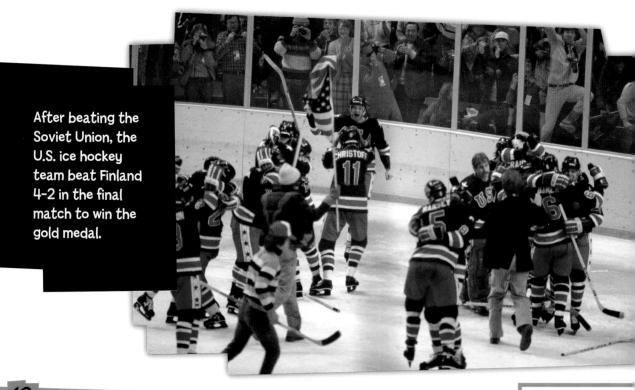

After beating the Soviet Union, the U.S. ice hockey team beat Finland 4–2 in the final match to win the gold medal.

"Eddie the Eagle"

At the Calgary Winter Olympics in 1988, Michael Edwards from the United Kingdom finished last in the ski jump competition. This was no surprise, as there were no ski jumps in the UK where he could practice. The surprise was that Edwards could compete at all. He became a hero for many who loved to see his obvious enthusiasm for the sport. They gave him the nickname "Eddie the Eagle."

Michael "Eddie the Eagle" Edwards in mid-air during one of his ski jumps at the 1988 Winter Olympics in Calgary, Canada.

Multiple Medalists

At the Olympics there have been some truly outstanding individual achievements. Some athletes are just happy to take part, which is what the Olympics are really all about. Others are thrilled to win a medal of any sort. Some athletes are determined to win gold again, and again, and again! Here are some famous Olympic champions:

Name: Jesse Owens
Born: 1913, Oakville, Alabama
Medals: Four gold
Jesse Owens was the first athlete to win four gold medals at a single Olympics.

Name: Fanny Blankers-Koen
Born: 1918, Baarn, Netherlands
Medals: Four gold
Dutch woman Fanny Blankers-Koen was the first woman to win four gold medals at a single Olympics when she competed in the 1948 London Olympic Games.

Name: Frederick Carlton Lewis (Carl Lewis)
Born: 1961, Birmingham, Alabama
Medals: Nine gold, one silver
Carl Lewis won four gold medals at the 1984 Olympics in Los Angeles.

Name: Mark Spitz
Born: 1950, Modesto, California
Medals: Nine gold, one silver, one bronze
In the 1972 Munich Olympics, swimmer Mark Spitz became the first person to win seven golds at a single Olympics.

Name: Mustapha Badid
Born: France
Medals: Five gold
At the 1988
Paralympic Games
in Seoul, South Korea,
wheelchair racer
Mustapha Badid won
four gold medals for
wheelchair racing.

Name: Ian Thorpe
Born: 1982, Sydney, New South Wales, Australia
Medals: Five gold, three silver, one bronze
Seventeen-year-old Australian swimmer Ian Thorpe gained
the nickname "Thorpedo" after winning three gold and
two silver medals at the 2000 Olympic Games in Sydney.

Name: Ole Einar Bjørndalen
Born: 1974, Drammen, Norway
Medals: Six gold, four silver, one bronze
Ole Einar Bjorndalen won four gold medals in the biathlon
at the 2002 Winter Olympics in Salt Lake City.

Name: Kelly Holmes
Born: 1970, Pembury, Kent, United Kingdom
Medals: Two gold, one bronze
When she won two gold medals in Athens in 2004, Kelly
Holmes became the first British woman since 1956 to win
multiple gold medals at a single Olympics.

Repeat Success

Winning a gold medal at one Olympics is special, but to win gold at **consecutive** Olympics is amazing. The following athletes have managed to achieve this incredible feat:

- Aladar Gerevich, from Hungary, won gold medals in fencing at six consecutive Olympics (1932, 1936, 1948, 1952, 1956, and 1960).

- Lasse Viren, a Finnish long distance runner, won gold medals in the 5,000-meter and 10,000-meter races at the 1972 and 1976 Olympic Games.

- Nadia Comaneci from Romania won multiple gold medals in gymnastics at the 1976 and 1980 Olympics.

U.S. sprinter Michael Johnson won gold in the 400-meter race at the 1996 and 2000 Olympics.

Czech gymnast Vera Caslavska took part in three Olympics. After winning a silver medal in 1960, she won three gold medals in 1964, and four more in 1968!

- Tanni Grey-Thompson won gold medals at four consecutive **Paralympic Games** (1992, 1996, 2000, and 2004).

- Steve Redgrave is the only British male athlete to win a gold medal at five consecutive Olympics. The British rower first won gold at the 1984 games in Los Angeles. He won his fifth and final gold medal at the 2000 Olympics in Sydney.

- U.S. swimmer Michael Phelps is a **phenomenon**! Phelps has won more gold medals than anyone else in Olympic history. He followed up his success in Athens in 2000, where he won six gold medals, by winning eight gold medals in Beijing in 2008.

- U.S. snowboarder Shaun White won gold in the **halfpipe** at the Winter Olympics in 2006 and 2010.

Fair Play at the Olympics

The motto of the Olympic Games is "*Cituis, Altius, Fortius.*" That translates from Latin as "Faster, Higher, Stronger." The motto was created by Pierre de Coubertin, the founder of the modern Olympics. The motto reminds all Olympic competitors that taking part and doing your best are just as important as winning. Athletes are expected to compete fairly and show respect to their rivals.

Lap of honor

At the 1992 Barcelona Olympics, the winner of the 10,000-meter race was Derartu Tulu from Ethiopia. Derartu was the first black African woman to win an Olympic gold medal. When she finished she waited at the line for Elana Meyer, who came second. Meyer is a white South African. The two women then set off together on a lap of honor. The image of one black and one white African running together to the crowd's applause was a special moment in history.

Derartu Tulu (left) and Elana Meyer hold hands as they take a lap of honor after their 10,000-meter race at the Olympics in Barcelona, Spain.

Rewarding fair play

The Olympic Fair Play committee was set up in 1964. The committee gives awards to competitors who show an outstanding example of sportsmanship.

Special award

In 1964, the first ever letter of congratulations for an Act of Fair Play was awarded to the Swedish rowers Lars Gunnar Kall and Stig Lienart Kall by the International Fair Play Committee. The rowers were in an Olympic race for the gold medal, but stopped to help other competitors whose boat had capsized.

Brazilian runner Vanderlei de Lima was awarded a Fair Play Trophy after a spectator pushed him during the 2004 Olympic marathon, ruining his chance of winning the race.

Shocking Olympic Moments

The Olympic Games have seen moments of great sporting achievement and created heroes around the world. Alongside this success, however, there have been some shocking events.

Drugs at the Olympics

Although the Olympics have produced some amazing athletic performances, some athletes have chosen to use drugs as a way to win. One of the most shocking moments in Olympic history happened in 1988. The winner of the 100-meter dash, Ben Johnson from Canada, was stripped of his gold medal. He had tested positive for a banned substance a few days after the event.

21st-century cheating

Today the problem of athletes using drugs to gain an advantage over their opponents continues. United States sprinter Marion Jones won three gold and two bronze medals at the 2000 Olympics in Sydney, Australia. She later had to return the medals because she admitted to using **performance-enhancing drugs**.

Drunk athlete

The first athlete to be **disqualified** for drug use was Swedish pentathlete Hans-Gunner Liljenwall in 1968. He was disqualified for excessive alcohol intake.

Ben Johnson celebrates winning the 100 meters at the Seoul Olympics in 1988. However, he was not smiling a few days later, after being stripped of the title.

Running on rat poison

Some athletes will do anything to win. U.S. athlete Thomas Hicks, winner of the 1904 Olympic **marathon**, admitted to using a mixture of egg whites, brandy, and strychnine to improve his performance. Strychnine is the main ingredient in rat poison!

Terrorism at the Olympics

At all major world sporting events the fear of a **terrorist** attack is never very far away. A lot of money is spent on security, and everything is done to ensure that the Olympic Games run smoothly. Sometimes, however, tragedy strikes.

Munich, 1972

During the 1972 Olympics, a group of eight Palestinian terrorists broke into the **Olympic Village**, where the athletes were staying. Their intention was to kidnap the Israeli athletes. The terrorists were armed and determined. **Negotiations** were held to try to bring the situation to a peaceful end. Unfortunately, they did not succeed, and the German police decided to raid the room where the Israelis were being held.

The raid went disastrously wrong. It ended with all the Israeli athletes being killed, along with five terrorists and one policeman. As a sign of respect the Games were suspended for 36 hours, and a memorial service was held in the main stadium. Sadly, the 1972 Olympics will always be remembered more for this awful incident than for the athletes' achievements.

Atlanta, 1996

In 1996 a bomb exploded during a concert held to celebrate the opening of the Atlanta Olympics. The bomb killed one person and injured more than 100 others. Despite this tragedy, the Olympic organizing committee decided to continue with the Games. This prevented the terrorists from achieving their aim of disrupting or stopping the Olympics.

A memorial service is held in the Olympic stadium in Munich for the Israeli athletes murdered by terrorists during the 1972 Olympics.

Olympic Boycotts

There have been several occasions when certain countries have decided to **boycott** (not attend) the Olympic Games.

Africans refuse to compete

In 1976, 22 African countries boycotted the Montreal Games to protest against the fact that New Zealand was taking part. The African nations were angry that New Zealand had toured South Africa to play rugby. At the time, South Africa had a policy of **apartheid**. This meant that black people had fewer rights than white people. Most countries around the world would not allow their sporting teams to visit South Africa in protest against apartheid.

United States boycotts Moscow

The United States boycotted the Moscow Olympics in 1980 because they were unhappy that the **Soviet Union** had invaded Afghanistan. The governments of Great Britain and Australia were also not happy with this situation, but they allowed their athletes to attend the games.

Anything you can do . . .

The Soviet Union and other **communist** countries, including Cuba and Bulgaria, boycotted the 1984 Olympics in Los Angeles, California. This was a direct response to the United States not attending the Moscow Olympics four years earlier.

Sports and politics

Sports and politics should not mix, but sometimes sports are used as a way of making a political point. Occasionally this happens when a government prevents athletes from competing at the Olympics. Hopefully, every country will allow their athletes to compete at the 2012 Olympics in London.

This photograph shows the opening ceremony for the 1980 Olympics in Moscow. The United States did not send a team to compete at the Moscow Olympics.

Olympic Timeline

1896 Athens, Greece
1900 Paris, France
1904 Saint Louis, Missouri
1908 London, UK
1912 Stockholm, Sweden
1920 Antwerp, Belgium
1924 Paris, France
1924 Chamonix, France (W)
1928 Amsterdam, Netherlands
1928 St. Moritz, Switzerland (W)
1932 Los Angeles, California
1932 Lake Placid, New York (W)
1936 Berlin, Germany
1936 Garmisch-Partenkirchen, Germany (W)
1948 London, UK
1948 St. Moritz, Switzerland (W)
1952 Helsinki, Finland
1952 Oslo, Norway (W)
1956 Melbourne, Australia
1956 Cortina, Italy (W)
1960 Rome, Italy
1960 Squaw Valley, California (W)
1964 Tokyo, Japan
1964 Innsbruck, Austria (W)

1904: Gold, silver, and bronze medals are given out for the first time.

1948: Hungarian athlete Karoly Takacs wins gold in the pistol event. During World War II he had his right arm blown off by a grenade. He taught himself to shoot with his left hand.

1900: Women compete for the first time. The first gold medal is won by the British tennis player Charlotte Cooper.

1936: First Olympics to be shown on television. It is seen on giant screens in cinemas in Germany.

1964: The Olympics are held in Asia for the first time.

1924: For the first time, the closing ceremony includes raising the flag of the current host nation, future host nation, and the **International Olympic Committee**.

1932: Electronic timing and photo finishes are introduced.

1896: U.S. athlete James Connolly becomes the first Olympic champion for his performance in the triple jump.

1960: Boxer Clement "Ike" Quartey from Ghana becomes the first black African to win an Olympic medal.

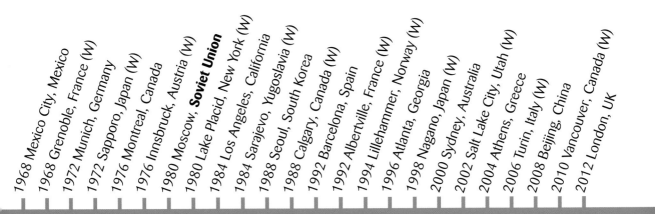

1968 Mexico City, Mexico
1968 Grenoble, France (W)
1972 Munich, Germany
1972 Sapporo, Japan (W)
1976 Montreal, Canada
1976 Innsbruck, Austria (W)
1980 Moscow, **Soviet Union**
1980 Lake Placid, New York (W)
1984 Los Angeles, California
1984 Sarajevo, Yugoslavia (W)
1988 Seoul, South Korea
1988 Calgary, Canada (W)
1992 Barcelona, Spain
1992 Albertville, France (W)
1994 Lillehammer, Norway (W)
1996 Atlanta, Georgia
1998 Nagano, Japan (W)
2000 Sydney, Australia
2002 Salt Lake City, Utah (W)
2004 Athens, Greece
2006 Turin, Italy (W)
2008 Beijing, China
2010 Vancouver, Canada (W)
2012 London, UK

1972: The Olympics are suspended for 36 hours after 11 Israeli athletes are murdered by Palestinian **terrorists**.

1984: American Carl Lewis wins four gold medals. He equals Jesse Owens's record from the 1936 Olympics.

1996: Austrian sailor Hubert Raudaschl becomes the first person to compete in nine Olympics.

2012: Olympics to be held in London for the first time since 1948.

1992: Professional athletes are allowed to compete at the Olympics for the first time.

1968: American Dick Fosbury changes the high jump forever by introducing a new jumping technique: the "Fosbury flop."

1980: Russian gymnast Aleksandr Dityatin becomes the first athlete to win eight medals at one Olympics: three gold, four silver, one bronze.

2008: U.S. swimmer Michael Phelps wins eight gold medals, breaking Mark Spitz's 36-year record.

2004: German Birgit Fischer becomes the first woman to win gold medals at six different Olympics.

Olympic Statistics

The Summer Olympics

Since the first Summer Olympic Games in 1896, there have been 26 Olympic Games held in 18 different countries. More than 100,000 athletes have taken part in the Olympics. Here are just a few interesting Olympic statistics:

- The United States has won more medals than any other country in Olympic history. U.S. athletes have won more than 2,300 medals.

- The youngest male athlete to win a medal at the Olympics was Greek gymnast Dimitrios Loundras. He was only ten years old when he won a bronze medal at the first Olympics in 1896.

- The oldest gold-medal winner in Olympic history is Oscar Swahn from Sweden. He won the shooting event at the 1920 Olympics. He was 72 years old!

- The youngest female medalist at the Olympics was 12-year-old breaststroke swimmer Inge Sorensen from Denmark. She won a bronze medal at the 1936 Olympics in Berlin.

- The youngest gold-medal-winning female athlete at the Olympics was American Marjorie Gestring. She was 13 years old when she won the diving competition in 1936.

The Winter Olympics

The first Winter Olympics were held in 1924, in Chamonix, France. Since then 21 Winter Olympic Games have been held in 10 different countries. More than 17,000 athletes from over 100 countries have taken part in the Winter Games, creating a wealth of statistics:

- Norway has won more Winter Olympic medals than any other country. Their athletes have won more than 300 medals.

- The youngest female athlete to compete at the Winter Olympics was British ice skater Cecillia Colledge. She was only 11 years old when she took part in 1932.

- The youngest female gold medallist is Kim Yung-Mi from South Korea. She was only 13 years old when she helped her team to win the 3,000-meter speed skating relay in 1994.

- Sweden finished second in the curling competition at the 1924 Winter Olympics. One member of the team was 58-year-old Carl August Krunland. He is the oldest medal winner in Winter Olympic history.

- Fifty-four-year-old British Robin Welsh Senior is the oldest Winter Olympic gold-medal winner. He won gold in the 1924 curling competition.

Glossary

ancient Greece several different city-states, including Athens and Sparta, that were in the area that is modern Greece more than 2,000 years ago

apartheid system that keeps people apart based on their skin color

boycott stay away from an event, often for political reasons

communist type of government where all people in a country share work and property

consecutive following one another in order

disqualify stop someone from being part of a race or competition because they have broken the rules

dominate to be in a commanding position

equality fairness; everyone being equal

halfpipe snowboarding event that takes place in a large area of snow cut in the shape of the bottom half of a pipe

International Olympic Committee (IOC) organization that runs the Olympic Games and decides where they will be held

marathon long running race held over 26.2 miles (42.2 kilometers)

negotiation attempt to reach an agreement by discussing something

Olympiad period of four years leading up to the Olympic Games

Olympic Village specially built housing where athletes and officials live during the Olympic Games

Paralympic Games games for athletes with a disability, held after the Olympic Games in the same place

performance-enhancing drug substance that is taken illegally to make an athlete faster and stronger

phenomenon something or someone that is out of the ordinary

segregation act of keeping two different things separate, in this case the black and white people in the United States.

Soviet Union state made up of Russia and several neighboring countries. The Soviet Union existed between 1922 and 1991.

terrorist person who uses violence against the public for political reasons

underdog person or team that is not expected to win

Find Out More

Books

Gifford, Clive. *Summer Olympics: The Definitive Guide to the World's Greatest Sports Celebration.* New York: Kingfisher, 2004.

Macy, Sue. *Freeze Frame: A Photographic History of the Winter Olympics.* Washington, D.C.: National Geographic Children's Books, 2006.

Olsen, Leigh. *Going for Gold: The 2008 U.S. Women's Gymnastics Team.* New York: Price Stern Sloan, 2008.

Page, Jason. *Basketball, Soccer, and other Ball Games* (The Olympic Sports). New York: Crabtree, 2008.

Zuehlke, Jeffrey. *Michael Phelps.* Minneapolis: Lerner Publications, 2009.

Websites

www.london2012.com
The website of the London 2012 Games includes details of venues and preparations for the Games, as well as information about Olympic sports.

www.olympic.org
The official website of the International Olympic Committee includes facts and statistics about every Olympic Games and every medal winner.

www.paralympic.org
This is the official website of the Paralympic movement.

To find out about the different countries competing at the Olympics, you can search for the National Olympic Committee of each country.

Index